D0382527

CH

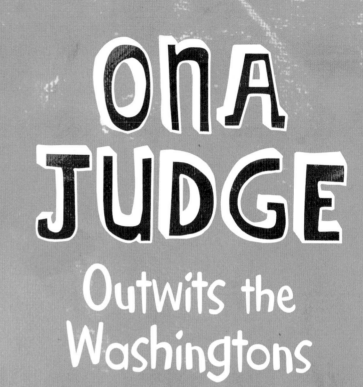

ONA JUDGE

Outwits the Washingtons

An Enslaved Woman Fights for Freedom

by Gwendolyn Hooks

illustrated by Simone Agoussoye

CAPSTONE EDITIONS
a capstone imprint

Young Ona Maria Judge was too little for housework. She had not grown strong enough for fieldwork. Instead she weeded, fed the chickens, and fetched water from the well.

Fetching water was not a safe job for a small child.

Ona would slowly lower the bucket deep down into the well.
She was careful not to lean over too far. If she fell in, there
would be no one to help her. The old folks who watched over
the young were too feeble for such a rescue.

Ona lived with her family on a Virginia plantation called Mount Vernon. They were all enslaved. Being enslaved meant they were considered legal property, like a mule or a cornfield. Ona and her family lived and worked in harsh conditions for no pay. Almost 700,000 other enslaved black people in the United States did too.

The enslaved people at Mount Vernon were the property of George and Martha Washington. General Washington was one of the most famous men in the United States. He was the commander of the Continental Army during the American Revolution.

American colonists fought the Revolutionary War against the British. The colonists won the right to make laws for themselves. At last, independence!

But nothing changed for Ona and most other enslaved people throughout the newly independent country. They would work for the rest of their lives for their slaveholders. If they displeased their owners, they were often sold to other slaveholders. Sometimes slaveholders sold children. Mothers and fathers stood helpless and heartbroken as their children disappeared down the road. They would never see one another again.

Ona knew life was a little easier inside the house than out in the fields. She hoped to work alongside her mother, Betty. Betty sewed for the Washington family. She also sewed and mended clothes for the enslaved people of the plantation.

Ona's little fingers were strong like her mother's. And she learned fast.

Ona was about ten years old the day Mrs. Washington sent for her. From then on, Ona would work inside the house with her mother.

She learned to spin thread and weave cloth. She sewed quick and steady stitches. She added elegant touches to Mrs. Washington's dresses. Even General Washington praised her skills. Most importantly, Ona could be near her mother while they worked.

One day a letter arrived. General Washington had been elected president of the United States. The letter from Congress declared that Washington had the support of the citizens of the United States—a "free and enlightened people."

Ona was taught nothing of freedom or enlightenment. She knew little about life beyond the plantation. Being curious or bright didn't matter. Ona was allowed to learn only about the work she was forced to do. Even if she was tired, hungry, or thirsty, Ona had to work and obey the Washingtons.

Mrs. Washington organized the move from Mount Vernon to the capital, New York City. Who should she take along? She knew they would need enslaved workers in their new home. The Washingtons picked those they felt were honest, smart, and not likely to run away.

Ona was chosen to go along. Her brother Austin and five other enslaved people were also chosen. In 1789, the Washingtons left Mount Vernon for their new home.

New York City dazzled Ona.
The streets bustled with foot
traffic and carriages. Ona lived
in the Presidential Mansion with
the Washingtons. The President
and Mrs. Washington paid white
servants to work for them. But
the enslaved workers received
no pay.

Ona helped Martha bathe. Ona
brushed Martha's hair. She repaired
and pressed Martha's dresses.

Ona was Martha's personal slave.
She accompanied her everywhere.
Ona rode a horse behind the
carriage that carried Martha
when she visited friends. She
went with Martha on sightseeing
trips around the city.

She kept Martha's fancy shoes
with the golden threads spotless.
At bedtime, she fetched Martha's
Bible for her nightly reading.

Ona had little time to herself. On Thursdays and Fridays, the Washingtons entertained their friends. These occasions were the only chance Ona had to relax and talk to Austin, the other enslaved people, and the white servants. Her conversations with them helped ease the pain she felt being away from the rest of her family. She couldn't wait to see them again.

President Washington soon grew tired of city life. He wanted to visit Mount Vernon. Ona was thrilled! They packed up the household and headed to Virginia.

Ona wanted to tell everyone about her life in the president's house. She worked with white servants. And she slept in the same house with them and the Washingtons. Ona worked hard in New York City. Her duties were tiresome. Still, she knew she was experiencing things the enslaved people at Mount Vernon never would.

Soon after they arrived home, Ona learned they would not return to New York City after all. Philadelphia, Pennsylvania, was the largest city in the United States and more centrally located than New York City. Philadelphia had been chosen to be the new capital and residence of the president.

Ona's new home would be near Independence Hall, where men had signed the Declaration of Independence and the U.S. Constitution. These important papers guaranteed rights and freedoms to citizens of the United States. But these documents did nothing for Ona. Because she was enslaved and treated as though she were property, she was not a citizen. For Ona, freedom was as far away as the moon.

In Philadelphia, Ona's days and nights continued much as they had in New York City. But the city itself was very different.

People in Pennsylvania had begun to argue against slavery. Free black people walked around Philadelphia. They went to churches. Ona was curious about their lives, but she was careful when she asked them questions. Others might think she was plotting to escape. She didn't want the president to hear that she'd been asking about freedom.

One day, Ona watched free black women selling pepperpot stew on the streets. The aroma of meat and peppers in a thick broth swirled around her. The women used whatever meat they could afford. Hard work showed on their faces. But every penny they earned was theirs to keep. They didn't call anyone master. They were free.

The women who stood before her proved freedom was possible.

If Ona escaped and was caught, she would be beaten. The Washingtons could sell her to a faraway owner. She would never see her family again. It was a frightening thought.

Ona knew the Washingtons would never set her free. To gain freedom, she would have to take the first step. Did she have the courage to run away?

In February 1796, Mrs. Washington received a surprising letter. Her granddaughter Elizabeth "Betsey" Parke Custis would soon marry. Martha had news for Ona: Ona would be their wedding gift!

Mrs. Washington's news crushed Ona's spirit. Ona knew Betsey well from her many visits to Mount Vernon. Could she bear Betsey's harsh demands and her cruel punishments?

The idea of living in Virginia sent shudders through Ona. In Philadelphia, Ona felt freedom was within reach. But Virginia was a solid slave state. Enslaved people in Virginia who tried to escape often faced bloody beatings or were sold.

It was time to act.

Ona saw her chance the day Richard Allen arrived at the president's home. Richard was a minister, a chimney sweep, and a free black man. The Washingtons hired him to clean soot from the chimneys. Ona took a risk and asked him to help her run away.

Reverend Allen agreed to help. He alerted his trusted circle of friends. They planned Ona's escape route leading north. They would tell Ona the plan one step at a time. Then if someone reported Ona, only one link in the chain of helpers would break. The others would be safe to help the next person seeking freedom.

Ona continued to work as hard as ever. The Washingtons had given her a few dollars to buy presents for her family. Ona saved some of the money for her journey. Between her tasks, she packed small bundles of clothes. She hid them with trusted friends.

One evening in May 1796, Ona quietly left the Presidential Mansion. She slipped out the door as the family ate supper. As instructed, she made her way to a secret place. Her heart pounded as she waited for the next step.

Ona knew President Washington would send people looking for her. She hoped he would not punish her family. But she would never go back to her life of slavery at Mount Vernon.

She didn't know what was ahead. But it would be better than what she left behind.

Her next step was a sea trip. Her friends arranged passage north aboard the *Nancy*, a ship commanded by Captain John Bowles.

After five days at sea, the *Nancy* docked in Portsmouth, New Hampshire. Ona would be forever thankful to Captain Bowles. If his part in her escape was ever found out, he could be sent to jail—or worse.

With jumbled nerves and a racing heart, Ona wrapped herself in courage. She stepped off the ship. She walked onto the land of her new home.

Ona searched the crowds for the family who would help her. What if she approached the wrong person and gave herself away? She'd be sent back to the Washingtons and face a horrible punishment. Just as her courage began to dip, a free black family stepped up and welcomed her to Portsmouth.

Her doubts turned into excitement. Ona quickly looked for a job. Runaways had to be careful. The skills that made her valuable to Mrs. Washington could also make others suspicious. People gossiped. News might travel back to Philadelphia about a black woman in New Hampshire who was talented with a needle and thread.

Instead Ona worked hard cleaning houses and cooking for white families. She didn't complain. Though she didn't earn much money, it was enough to live on with a little left over.

For the first time in her life, Ona's time belonged to her. She explored her new city. Portsmouth was smaller than Philadelphia and New York City, but it had a busy seaport. Ship builders thrived in Portsmouth. Captains delivered food and supplies up and down the Atlantic coast. Ona marveled at the items for sale in shop windows. She pictured buying them with her own money.

Ona enjoyed the salty air. To her it became the smell of freedom. She began to relax. But to relax completely was dangerous.

No matter how careful Ona was, some things were out of her control. One day as she walked down the street, she saw a woman who looked familiar. The woman's name was Elizabeth Langdon. She and her family had been frequent visitors to the Presidential Mansion.

Ona froze with fear. Maybe Elizabeth wouldn't recognize her. Ona pretended she didn't see her and kept walking.

But Elizabeth recognized Ona. The young woman hurried
home and promptly told her father about the odd sighting.
Her father, a senator, informed President Washington that his
runaway slave was in Portsmouth.

President Washington plotted Ona's return. He hired Joseph Whipple, the customs collector in Portsmouth, to find Ona and force her back to Philadelphia. Whipple tried to trick Ona. He lured her with news of a job. Ona met with him but realized there was no job. He wanted her to return to the Washingtons.

Ona knew it was not wise to anger this man, so she agreed to sail back to Philadelphia. But she had a trick of her own.

Whipple waited at the dock for Ona. She never came. The Washingtons were furious when they heard. But President Washington was about to retire after two terms. Making Ona return by force would cause bad publicity. He did not want to end his presidency with a runaway slave scandal in the newspapers.

Meanwhile in Portsmouth, Ona met a free black man named Jack Staines. He worked on a ship and sailed away for months at a time. They fell in love.

But when they applied for a marriage certificate, Whipple turned up again. He had not forgotten his duty to the president. He couldn't force Ona back to the Washingtons, but he could make her life difficult. Whipple used his power to delay the marriage paperwork.

It didn't stop Ona and Jack. They applied for a certificate in Greenland, a neighboring town. Ona and Jack were legally married January 14, 1797.

The next year Ona and Jack had a baby daughter, Eliza. Ona continued to work hard and help earn money. Slowly, her worries faded, and she began to enjoy her life. Under law she was still enslaved. But she lived her life as though she was a free woman.

President Washington, however, could not forget the slave who had outwitted him. He and Mrs. Washington still fumed over Ona's escape. They wanted her back.

One night, while Jack was away at sea, Ona and baby Eliza had an unexpected visitor. It was Burwell Bassett, Mrs. Washington's nephew. Ona recognized him right away. She had seen him many times in the Washington home.

Ona knew why he was at her door. The Washingtons had not given up. Bassett said the Washingtons would grant her freedom if only she would return to Mount Vernon.

Ona knew better. She stood her ground and refused to go with him.

Bassett was just as stubborn as Ona. He couldn't believe that a slave would refuse to obey him. He hatched another plot. This time Bassett planned to kidnap Ona. He was visiting the Langdons and discussed his plan. One of the Langdons' servants overheard Bassett talking and told Ona.

Ona acted quickly. She packed her family's belongings and wrapped baby Eliza in a warm blanket. Then she hurried to find a driver with a horse and carriage. They sped toward Greenland. A free black family took them in. The family watched over them until Jack returned home.

Once Jack arrived home, Ona and her family settled in Greenland. Under the law, Ona Maria Judge Staines remained a runaway for the rest of her life. Not even the president of the United States could convince Ona to go back to Mount Vernon. Ona had carved out a life of her own where she answered to no master but herself.

A newspaper reporter once asked if Ona regretted the hard life she'd led.

"No," she said, "I am free. . . ."

Author's Note: Hidden in Plain View

As I began reading about Ona Maria Judge Staines, I couldn't believe what I found. A young enslaved woman escaped from President George Washington, and he couldn't get her back? I was hooked. I had to learn more. I have presented the information about Ona's life to the best of my research, even though some sources differ in their accounts.

In the book, I use the term *enslaved* instead of *slave*. A person did not *decide* to become a slave like someone decides to become a teacher. Enslaved people did not have choices. Plantation owners forced them to work for the rest of their lives without pay. They were enslaved.

The practice of enslavement dates back hundreds of years—long before George Washington became president. Slave hunters kidnapped men, women, and children from Africa. They chained and crowded them onto ships bound for what is now the United States.

When the ships arrived, plantation and farm owners bought these kidnapped people to work for them. Enslaved families did not always stay together. They worked from sunup to sundown. Sunday was usually a rest day. Owners forbid them to learn to read and write.

Ona had a last name, which most enslaved did not. Ona's father, Andrew Judge, was a white indentured servant from England. He signed a contract to work on Mount Vernon for four years. He was a tailor. He sewed clothes for the Washington family. After four years, he was free to leave. Ona never heard from her father again. But he left her with a middle and last name.

Ona did have some freedoms most enslaved could not imagine. Ona accompanied Mrs. Washington when she visited her friends. Ona wore pretty dresses and shoes. The Washingtons gave her money for shopping trips. She attended plays and circus performances.

In Philadelphia, Ona's spirit grew bolder. Despite the danger, she sailed north. Ona struggled for the rest of her life. She outlived her husband and three children. She never saw her Mount Vernon family again. But Ona Maria Judge Staines lived life on her terms.

—Gwendolyn Hooks

Read More

Delano, Marfe Ferguson. *Master George's People: George Washington, His Slaves, and His Revolutionary Transformation.* Washington, D.C.: National Geographic, 2013.

Kimmel, Allison Crotzer. *A Primary Source History of Slavery in the United States.* Primary Source History. North Mankato, MN: Capstone Press, 2015.

Levy, Janey. *Slavery at Mount Vernon.* Hidden History. New York: Gareth Stevens Publishing, 2017.

About the Author

Gwendolyn Hooks has written many books, including *If You Were a Kid During the Civil Rights Movement*, *The Cat Food Mystery*, and *Tiny Stitches: The Life of Medical Pioneer Vivien Thomas*, for which she received the NAACP Image Award for Outstanding Children's Literature. She is the recipient of the Society of Children's Book Writers and Illustrators Crystal Kite Award, and her book *Block Party* is a Junior Library Guide selection. Gwendolyn resides in Oklahoma City, Oklahoma.

About the Illustrator

Simone Agoussoye is an artist who has been drawing and painting since she was a little girl. Art has always been an outlet for Simone, and by third grade, she knew exactly what she wanted to be when she grew up—an artist. Simone's work incorporates color, nature, and emotion. She enjoys drawing and painting portraits most of all. Simone lives and works in Baltimore, Maryland.

Ona Judge Outwits the Washingtons is published by
Capstone Editions, a Capstone imprint
1710 Roe Crest Drive, North Mankato, Minnesota 56003
www.mycapstone.com

Copyright © 2019 Capstone Editions

Library of Congress Cataloging-in-Publication Data
Names: Hooks, Gwendolyn, author. | Agoussoye, Simone, illustrator.
Title: Ona Judge outwits the Washingtons : an enslaved woman fights for
   freedom / by Gwendolyn Hooks ; illustrated by Simone Agoussoye.
Description: North Mankato, Minnesota : Capstone Editions, [2019] | Series:
   Capstone editions. Encounter: narrative nonfiction picture books |
   Audience: Ages 9-12.
Identifiers: LCCN 2018029009 (print) | LCCN 2018030743 (ebook) | ISBN
   9781543512885 (eBook PDF) | ISBN 9781543512809 (hardcover)
Subjects: LCSH: Judge, Oney. | Slaves—United States—Biography—Juvenile
   literature. | Washington, George, 1732-1799—Relations with
   slaves—Juvenile literature. | Washington, Martha, 1731-1802—Relations
   with slaves—Juvenile literature. | African American
   women—Biography—Juvenile literature. | Fugitive slaves—United
   States—Biography—Juvenile literature. |
   Slavery—Pennsylvania—Philadelphia—History—18th century—Juvenile
   literature.
Classification: LCC E444.J83 (ebook) | LCC E444.J83 H66 2019 (print) | DDC
   306.3/62092 [B] —dc23
LC record available at https://lccn.loc.gov/2018029009

Direct Quotation:
Page 36: Adams, Rev. T H. "Washington's Runaway Slave." *The Granite
Freeman*, May 22, 1845. Accessed Dec. 27, 2018, http://www.ushistory.org/
presidentshouse/slaves/oneyinterview.php.

Thanks to our adviser for her expertise, research, and advice:
Dr. Catherine Adams
Associate Professor of History
The State University of New York–Geneseo

Designers: Ashlee Suker and Nathan Gassman

All internet sites appearing in back matter were available and accurate when this book was sent to press.

Printed and bound in China.
001670

Selected Bibliography

Adams, Rev. T H. "Washington's Runaway Slave." *The Granite Freeman*, May 22, 1845. Accessed Dec. 27, 2018, http://www.ushistory.org/presidentshouse/slaves/oneyinterview.php.

Bryan, Helen. *Martha Washington: First Lady of Liberty*. New York: Wiley, 2002.

Casey, Michael. "Ona Judge: The Slave Who Ran Away from George Washington." *U.S. News & World Report*, Oct. 04, 2017. Accessed Dec. 27, 2018, https://www.usnews.com/news/best-states/new-hampshire/articles/2017-10-04/ona-judge-the-slave-who-ran-away-from-george-washington.

Chase, Rev. Benjamin. "Letter to the editor." *The Liberator*, Jan. 01, 1847. Accessed Dec. 27, 2018, http://www.ushistory.org/presidentshouse/slaves/oneyinterview.php.

Dunbar, Erica Armstrong. *Never Caught: The Washingtons' Relentless Pursuit of Their Runaway Slave, Ona Judge*. New York: 37 Ink/Atria, 2017.

"George Washington's Mount Vernon." Mount Vernon Ladies' Association. Accessed Dec. 26, 2018, https://www.mountvernon.org/.

Wiencek, Henry. *An Imperfect God: George Washington, His Slaves, and the Creation of America*. New York: Farrar, Straus and Giroux, 2003.